<u>**The G**</u>

All Scripture references from the English Standard Version - Crossway Publications unless otherwise noted.

The Holy Bible, English Standard Version® (ESV®)
Copyright © 2001 by Crossway,
a publishing ministry of Good News Publishers.
All rights reserved.
ESV Text Edition: 2007

ISBN: 978-1-304-90881-0

Dedication

To my Dad, the Rev. Raymond F. Ferguson

Who baptized me upon my confession of faith when I was but 8 years old.

And who shepherded my soul from the pulpit and in the home, that I might love God's Word, the Gospel, the Christ who gave Himself for us, and who taught me to pray.

The Gift of Believer's Baptism

PART I

Matthew 28:19-20

> *"Go therefore and make disciples of all nations, baptizing them in the name of the Father and of the Son and of the Holy Spirit, [20]teaching them to observe all that I have commanded you. And behold, I am with you always, to the end of the age."* **Matthew 28:19–20**

If you are reading this to in order to answer the question for yourself - "should I be baptized?" - Great! You are in the right place. That is precisely why this book has been put together. Or you may be reading it just to inform yourself better on the topic, or to help someone else work through their own questions on water baptism. Either way, welcome.

Before we get too far down the road however, it might be good to consider the short answer to the question above - before we attempt to answer it more fully.

And the short answer is: It depends. How's that for being equivocal?

There are several reasons why we answer that way.

The fact is, in light of what The Bible says about water baptism, some who have been baptized never ought to have been; some think they have been baptized when they really haven't; some should be baptized who never have been; and none should be baptized until they are Biblically eligible to be baptized.

It sounds complicated at first, but it truly isn't. We just need to grasp some fundamentals from the Scripture in order to arrive the right answer.

I. THE COMMAND

The text we cited at the very beginning is a great place to start. Once again it reads -

> *"Go therefore and make disciples of all nations, baptizing them in the name of the Father and of the Son and of the Holy Spirit, ^{20}teaching them to observe all that I have commanded you. And behold, I am with you always, to the end of the age."* **Matthew 28:19–20**

The basic message of the passage is pretty clear right off the bat - Go make disciples of Jesus – based upon Jesus' supreme authority (vs. 18). And that making of disciples is accomplished in two parts:

> a. Baptizing them with the authority of the Triune God, (i.e. in the "name" of the Father and of the Son and of the Holy Spirit - acting on their behalf, as their authorized agents)

> b. Teaching them to observe all that I have commanded you.

Along with this, Jesus promises that He attends this activity personally - and will do so right up to the end of time. This establishes His wonderfully concise command both in regard to the commission to the Apostles, and to the Church at large in the ages to come after the Apostles.

With all the rest of the dust blown off then – we can see that a primary focus of the church is to be: "Making disciples of all nations."

Parallel to the passage already cited is Mark 16:15–16, where we read:

> *"And he said to them, "Go into all the world and proclaim the gospel to the whole creation. Whoever believes and is baptized will be saved, but whoever does not believe will be condemned."* **Mark 16:15-16**

It is useful to put this passage alongside of the other one so that we can see that it is NOT lack of being BAPTIZED that condemns a person - it is lack of BELIEVING. Unfortunately, there has been a lot of (unnecessary) confusion on that point. Confusion we want to clear up before moving on.

Water baptism saves no one. We are delivered from God's just wrath - which is to come upon the whole world - through faith in the person and work of Jesus Christ; in His life of perfect righteousness, and His atoning, substitutionary death on the Cross - alone. That doesn't mean baptism isn't important. By virtue of Christ's command to do it, we can clearly see it is. However, it is not THE most important thing. As the Holy Spirit said through the Apostle Paul:

> *"But if it is by grace, it is no longer on the basis of works; otherwise grace would no longer be grace."* **Romans 11:6**

In other words, there is no "work" or activity which can save us. Salvation is rooted in the free gift of God's grace received through faith - and expressly NOT by works of any kind. (Rom. 3:21-26)

Nevertheless baptism is not unimportant, and in fact is linked to believing in a powerful way. We'll see more of that as we move further along.

Let's recap using both passages:

The making of disciples is located chiefly in 3 things:

>1. In preaching the Gospel to the whole creation

And then based upon believing it,

>2. Those who believe are to be baptized

And then

>3. The baptized are to be taught to observe all that Christ had commanded.

II. DISCIPLES

It might be helpful at this point to define just what a "disciple" is to help us better understand what baptism and being taught to observe Christ's commands have to do with it.

In the language of the New Testament (Greek) the word "disciples" carries a number of informative meanings. Hearers; Followers of; Students of; Emissaries of - and several others. All of which play into carrying on Christ's work and purposes in this present world.

No one (in Biblical thought) is simply a "believer" but not a disciple. Believers are those who take Jesus Christ as their Lord (the authority over their persons and lives) and so give themselves to learning about Him, what He said and why He said it; who He is and what He has done, and what He is accomplishing in this world He has created. Seeking to know and be a part of His accomplishing His eternal goals in creation and in salvation. What He is going about doing and accomplishing. Whenever Jesus called disciples to Himself, that call was always to "follow me." And what an unspeakable privilege that is.

Now the fact that our text puts being baptized and being taught to observe what Jesus has commanded in that order, does not ignore that some teaching goes on before baptism. People need to know why they ought to want to be baptized before they are. But our learning does not end after one has been baptized either. As disciples - we go on learning, it becomes our lifelong vocation. We are now followers, disciples of Christ Jesus.

The Gospel itself is pretty straightforward. We can go to any number of passages where it is given to us in varying and explicit terms. One of the most succinct in this regard is in what our Bibles contain as Paul's first letter to the church in the ancient city of Corinth:

> *"Now I would remind you, brothers, of the gospel I preached to you, which you received, in which you stand, ²and by which you are being saved, if you hold fast to the word I preached to you—unless you believed in vain. ³For I delivered to you as of first importance what I also received: that Christ died for our sins in accordance with the Scriptures, ⁴that he was buried, that he was raised on the third day in accordance with the Scriptures, ⁵and that he appeared to Cephas, then to the twelve."*
> **1 Corinthians 15:1–5**

As to teaching the Believers whatsoever Christ had commanded us (Matt. 28:20) – we have the four Gospels themselves, and their continued explanation and application in the rest of the epistles.

Added to those we have these Gospel concepts graphically displayed in the Old Testament as a sort of illustration book. This is why we teach the entire Bible as an integrated whole.

It is interesting to note however, that there is no one passage in the Bible that completely and simply unpacks this idea of baptism in and of itself - the way one like the 1 Corinthians passage does the Gospel.

For this, we are forced (by design no doubt) to search out all the various passages which refer to and demonstrate baptism, and construct from those passages the meaning and importance of baptism.

III. INSIGHT ON BAPTISM FROM THE REST OF THE BIBLE

It is interesting to note that water baptism (even by immersion) was not unknown to the Jewish nation before John the Baptizer came on the scene. But there were only 4 cases scripturally where it was required, and one more that developed in Jewish practice over time.

The first time we see an early picture of baptism is found in the book of Leviticus.

a. In the case of a leper being restored after being cured. In order for a leper to be readmitted to the community (Lev. 14) he or she needed to (among other things) be fully "bathed" in water (or baptized) as a sign of their being cleansed.

b. In Leviticus 15, we see this same idea repeated for those who had become ceremonially unclean by defilement of other kinds. And in this case it was a rite repeated as needed. It wasn't done once for all time.

c. When the High Priest was ordained into office is another occasion. And this was repeated by him in preparation on the Day of Atonement - so that he might safely appear before God in the Holy of Holies. (Lev. 16) This "baptism" on the Day of Atonement was repeated yearly.

d. Also connected with the ceremonies on the Day of Atonement, was the baptism of the man who led the atonement goat into the wilderness that day. (Lev. 16) This too was repeated annually.

e. Lastly, though this is not mentioned in Scripture, we know that by Jesus' time a full immersion baptism was required of any proselyte - or one who was a convert to Judaism. This would have been done only once, at their initial entrance into the community.

IV. A COMMON MISCONCEPTION

Before we go too much further, it might be good to address a common **mis**conception among some Christians, that baptism replaced circumcision as the initiatory rite into the believing community. Due to this line of reasoning, infant baptism (also called paedobaptism) was initially introduced to the Church even before the more modern idea of "covenant baptism" was minted. [1]

---

[1] We want to be very careful here and note that infant baptism as practiced in the vast majority of Reformed and Calvinistic churches is NOT considered salvific in and of itself. Those holding to the Westminster standards do not teach what is termed "baptismal regeneration" – i.e. that baptism saves the child or makes them justified before God. They practice what is referred to as "covenant baptism" meaning that the child, by virtue of being born to believing parents is considered a part of the larger "covenant community" and therefore ought to bear the "sign and seal" of the covenant (baptism) in the hope and anticipation of (perhaps even the presumption of) their future justification by faith. And it is this form of infant baptism we will be arguing against in this book - not the aberrant forms of infant baptism which claim that the child is actually saved or justified before God simply by being baptized. For the best explanation and defense of covenant baptism this author is aware of - see Dr. Kenneth Talbot's fine work: "Confirming our Faith: A Reformed Covenantal Theology of the Sacraments." See Appendix C.

In contrast, Roman Catholic infant baptism supposes an "infusion" of grace into the child. In their thought, the rite itself creates spiritual life in the infant. For all intents and purposes the child is a "Christian" in right standing before God at that point.

Our stance on that would be in agreement with what we find in the New Bible Dictionary article on baptism where we read:

> "More to the point is Paul's argument against the necessity of circumcision, despite the explicit warnings of Gn. 17:9–14. What mattered was the circumcision 'made without hands' (Col. 2:11—hardly a description of baptism), the circumcision of the heart (Rom. 2:28–29), which the gift of the Spirit effected (Phil. 3:3). In fact it was the presence of the Spirit which defined the Christian (Rom. 8:9 em; the nearest definition of a Christian in the NT). Reception of the Spirit rendered circumcision unnecessary (Gal. 3:3; 5:3–5; Rom. 2:28–29). For Paul, the Spirit had replaced circumcision as the hallmark of the covenant people (2 Cor. 3:3, 6), the evidence of the Spirit in a person's life serving as a sign and seal of the new covenant just as circumcision served for the old covenant (Jer. 31:31–34; 2 Cor. 1:22; *cf.* Rom. 4:11).[2]"

In other words, physical circumcision is replaced in the New Covenant by the circumcision of the heart - through the giving of the Holy Spirit, not by baptism. (See: Romans 2:28-29)

The lack of any explicit example of an infant being baptized in the New Testament, nor of any command for infants to be baptized, and the linking of baptism in every account of baptism in the New Testament with prior faith and/or believing - leads us to hold to a

---

However, this "grace" can be sinned away by virtue of committing mortal sins (mortal because they "kill" the grace infused at baptism) and which can then be subsequently restored through various rites, rituals and sacraments. This view we would consider as heretical.

[2] Wood, D. R. W., & Marshall, I. H. (1996). *New Bible dictionary* (3rd ed.) (121). Leicester, England; Downers Grove, IL: InterVarsity Press.

"believers only" baptism. This then precludes infants from being baptized, as they do not yet believe the Gospel.[3]

V. AN OBSERVATION

In our day, baptism has fallen on hard times. Sadly, seldom is much emphasis put upon it by the Church in many circles.

A few reasons as to why this may be the case are -

a. A lack of clear teaching on the importance of baptism. Or more importantly, lack of teaching on the privilege and honor of baptism.

b. The fact that in a free society like our own, the impact of a public display of one's unity with Christ and His people is no longer costly for most of us and so it loses its impact. In the first centuries of the Church especially, being baptized as a public display of one's trust in Jesus Christ could get a Jew banned from their Synagogue, or even imprisoned or punished. Such persecution grew from only Jewish persecution to Roman persecution. And in countless numbers of cases historically, being baptized as a disciple of Jesus Christ could cost one their life. The loss of those realities can, in the first place, make baptism more reasonable to those who are not truly committed to following Christ for the long haul, and, in the second place dull its importance over all.

c. It seems old and antiquated. And let's face it, it DOES seem old and antiquated. Especially if one has no idea that Jesus actually commanded it, and why.

---

[3] See part 2 of this book for a fuller treatment regarding Biblical reasons for rejecting infant baptism.

d. We seem to hear very little today of the sweet gift baptism is intended to be to us from our God - like a priceless engagement ring to His betrothed.

e. It seems likely that a large portion of the problem can be located in the way our present culture fragments almost every institution. It is the modern problem of atomistic thinking which is so prevalent in American culture today.

Atomistic thinking divides things into their separate parts, so as to lose the reality and benefit of the whole. So in our day things like sex and marriage have been separated as though you can have the individual parts, without the whole. A completely contrary view to that of Scripture.

Scripture knows of no legitimate sexual relationship between two people apart from the context of marriage. But our culture has seen the two parts and concluded they do not need to be welded together as God intends, but can be had separately.

The whole requires both parts and both parts form the whole.

In the same way we have people claiming they have Jesus as their Savior, but not as their Lord. This is a kind of aberrant division the Scripture knows nothing about.

Additionally, this kind of atomistic thinking invites other strange ideas like; Christianity without the Church, or Christianity without the Bible or public worship, or the Lord's Supper or - BAPTISM! etc.

If we approach baptism atomistically, or something else, like communion (the Lord's Supper) in similar ways to our culture - by making them mere individual electives instead of the sweet blessings they are meant to be as part of experiencing the whole of the Christian life and witness - we miss the beauty and importance of them altogether.

VI - THINKING OF BAPTISM BIBLICALLY

Let's try to get at the big picture on baptism by considering three areas:

I – What baptism SYMBOLIZES – What it explains to us

II – What baptism DEMONSTRATES – What it shows us

III – What baptism DECLARES – What it says by our participation in it.

I - What baptism SYMBOLIZES – What it explains to us by way of representation.

1. Baptism Symbolizes FORGIVENESS

The Biblical view of mankind begins with our being created upright and holy "in the image of God". (Genesis 1 & 2) But it wasn't very long before we fell. Hard. Adam and Eve (the whole human race at that time) rebelled against God by disobeying Him in regard to eating the forbidden fruit in Eden. (Genesis 3) And so as a race, we transgressed God's law together. All of human suffering and misery has resulted from that rebellion. This is why we (as a race) need the forgiveness of the God we rejected back then.

But that is not the end of the story. Added to the rebellion of Adam and Eve, are the personal, individual sins you and I (and every other human being) also commit. Being both sinners by virtue of our connection with Adam and Eve and as sinners still sinning - we are separated from the God who made us, and desperately need His forgiveness to be reconciled to Him. This is at the heart of the

Bible and of the Gospel. For in the Gospel, the way God has made for us to be forgiven - is through believing in His Son Jesus Christ. It is just as it is in human relationships. When we've offended one another, we seek the offended person's forgiveness so that we can restore our relationship. Sinners need God's forgiveness, so that we can be restored to a right relationship to Him too.

So it is the Bible employs different terms and pictures to help us grasp the forgiveness He offers us in the person and work of Jesus.

When someone forgives a debt for instance, the one doing the forgiving (metaphorically) stamps our bill "PAID IN FULL" - meaning the debt is forgiven and doesn't need to be repaid anymore.

But the picture of our guilt and need for forgiveness in the Bible also includes the aspect of our being defiled. Stained. That we are in some way "unclean" and need not just to be forgiven, but forgiven in a way that removes the mark from our record completely. After all, it is one thing to forgive someone who has stolen money so that they will not be punished or have to pay it back - but quite another to take away the mark that has been put on their record branding them as a thief! How does one do that? How does one become "not guilty" after the fact?

The Bible says that is precisely what the blood of Jesus does for us. When we humble ourselves before Him, confessing our sin and seeking His forgiveness, in the words of **1 John 1:7** - *"the blood of His Son Jesus cleanses us from all sin."*

And this idea of cleansing and forgiveness is repeated throughout the Scripture. One notable place is Ezekiel 36 where God promises forgiveness to His people Israel in these words:

> **Ezekiel 36:24–29** *"I will take you from the nations and gather you from all the countries and bring you into your own land. I will sprinkle clean water on you, and you shall be clean from all your uncleannesses, and from all your idols I will*

> *cleanse you. And I will give you a new heart, and a new spirit I will put within you. And I will remove the heart of stone from your flesh and give you a heart of flesh. And I will put my Spirit within you, and cause you to walk in my statutes and be careful to obey my rules. You shall dwell in the land that I gave to your fathers, and you shall be my people, and I will be your God. And I will deliver you from all your uncleannesses. And I will summon the grain and make it abundant and lay no famine upon you.*

Baptism - as it is a washing, symbolizes these very truths - how God promises to give His Spirit to us, and to wash us and take away all of our uncleanness due to our sin. What a picture!

Christian, when you get baptized, you are physically acting out what God has done by His Spirit when you believed the Gospel. You were washed clean by Him. And the stains of those old, forgiven sins, are wiped away forever. He gives you baptism to cement those realities in your heart and mind so that you know it is done. It is a symbol of your justification - being declared righteous before God.

2. Baptism Symbolizes ACCEPTANCE

Jesus, we are told in John 14:1 is the "**only** Son of the Father" (or the **only** "begotten" Son in some versions), and yet in **1 John 3:1–2** we read:

> *"See what kind of love the Father has given to us, that we should be called children of God; and so we are. The reason why the world does not know us is that it did not know him. Beloved, we are God's children now, and what we will be has not yet*

> *appeared; but we know that when he appears we shall be like him, because we shall see him as he is."*

So is Jesus the **only** Son, or are believers sons too? How are we supposed to make sense of those two things? The answer is to be found in the reality that there are two ways one can become a son or daughter of someone.

The first is by natural means like birth - by physically issuing from the parents themselves. This is the picture (an analogy - though not a perfect one) of the nature of Jesus' relationship to God the Father. They share the very same divinity. Jesus is both God and man, and eternally existed with the Father. They share one common life. Yet one is the Father, and the other is the Son and they interact in this relationship. But as we have seen – Jesus is the ONLY Son in this sense - the only "begotten" Son.

The second way one can become the true child of another, is through adoption. This precious figure is the one the Bible applies to believers. So we read in Romans (8 & 9), Galatians (4:5) and Ephesians (1:5) that when believers are born again by the Spirit, the Spirit indwelling us is the "Spirit of adoption" who allows us to cry out to God "Father" – as rightfully as Jesus does. For adopted children have no less rights than the natural children do. They are each full heirs.

It is with this in mind that Jesus models this concept for us Himself when He is baptized (Matthew 3) and a voice from heaven declares "this is my beloved Son, in whom I am well pleased."

As Jesus was announced to the world as the Son when He was baptized, so in our being baptized like Him we receive in that baptism a similar declaration of our adoption as children by the Father. It is like the sealing of the court papers declaring it a finished fact, and we are now in this unbreakable relationship to the Father. How amazing!

3. Baptism Symbolizes DEATH, BURIAL & RESURRECTION

One of the most profound things baptism does is to be seen in how it symbolizes our being joined to Christ, in all that He did for us in dying for our sins, being buried, and being raised up on the 3rd day so as to rise to the Father and pour out the Holy Spirit on believers.

Romans 6:3 & 4 is extremely helpful in opening these ideas up to us. There we read:

> *"Do you not know that all of us who have been baptized into Christ Jesus were baptized into his death?"*

And what else can symbolize death, burial and resurrection like entering the waters of baptism, being laid down or immersed, and then coming up again to walk in new life? The parallels are simply too graphic, stunning and precious to be ignored.

In this Romans passage, we are introduced to one of the best weapons a Christian has against temptation and indwelling sin through the symbolism of baptism. Paul here notes how water baptism is a link to what it means to be "joined" to Christ. Just as is also mentioned in 1 Corinthians (12:13 *for in one Spirit we were all baptized into one body—Jews or Greeks, slaves or free—and all were made to drink of one Spirit.* See also vs. 17), since by the Spirit we are made "one with Him" – certain things of His also become ours.

If that is so - if that is the nature of our salvation - then we have the benefit of all He did on our behalf acting as our representative - and what He did was die for our sin, was buried for our sin, and was raised for our justification!

> **Romans 6:6-7** *" We know that our old self was crucified with him in order that the body of sin might be brought to nothing, so that we would no*

longer be enslaved to sin. For one who has died has been set free from sin."

Because this is true, when we are tempted, it is an invaluable tool to recall our baptism so as to reinforce that we no longer HAVE to obey sin like we used to - for our baptism reminds us that in union with Christ - we HAVE DIED TO SIN so that we may be free, and have been RAISED WITH HIM so that we can walk in newness of life!

The baptized believer can say: "Wait a minute sin! I don't have to yield to you anymore like I used to. I am IN Christ. And I went into the waters of baptism to show that. And if I am in Him, I am no longer chained to serving you! I'M FREE!"

What an incredible weapon against the enemy who is always trying to deceive us that we cannot overcome our sin, but must just live in perpetual misery and slavery.

This is one of the reasons why baptism is so important for the everyday life of the believer. It enables us to fight the single most prevalent and continuous battle we have - against the pervasive lies of indwelling sin seeking to re-establish its rule over us.

II – What baptism DEMONSTRATES – What it shows us in action.

1. Baptism is a Demonstration of OBEDIENCE to The Lord of life

Since Jesus commanded the Church to be doing it, baptism becomes one of the most basic and primary acts of our submission to Him as the Lord – the supreme authority – over our lives.

When we look back at our core text, we are reminded that the Church is called to make disciples by baptizing them, and believers then are to be baptized. All at the behest of our Savior. The Church demonstrates its obedience to Jesus in making and baptizing disciples, and the disciples demonstrate their obedience in following their Lord's command. It is a public demonstration to the world that we have moved from obeying ourselves (or anyone else) as the supreme authority in all things, to obeying Jesus as the supreme authority in all things.

Let's face it, talk is cheap. Anyone can claim to be a follower of Jesus Christ. But the question is - are we actually following Him? Or are we just giving lip service to it? To follow Him, is to obey Him. And here, He gives us an extremely simple command. And make no mistake, it is out of step with the modern world and those outside of faith in Christ. But that is part of what makes it special. Here is a way that we demonstrate at the very outset of our profession of faith in Him and our claim to be His disciples - that when He asks such things of us - we respond.

In the Old Testament (2 Kings 5) we have the account of a Syrian military official, Naaman, who had contracted leprosy. In a raid on Israel, he also had acquired a young Jewish girl as a handmaid for his wife. When he came down with the dread disease, the little girl lamented his condition and expressed a wish that he could be in contact with a prophet in Israel who no doubt could heal him. As a valued soldier, the King gave Naaman leave to seek treatment if he could. So Naaman sought out the prophet Elisha.

When Naaman's entourage arrived at Elisha's door, Elisha never even came out to meet him. He told his servants to tell Naaman to go wash in the Jordan River 7 times and he would be well. Naaman was offended by what he perceived as a slight. What? No ceremony? No waving of the hands or chanting or anything? And besides he argued - "we've got rivers back in Syria I could bathe in if all I need is a bath." (Paraphrased) He was steaming mad and was going to just leave.

At that point, Naaman's faithful servants said to him - "look, isn't this amazing? All he said to you was go down and wash and you'd be clean!" Implying "don't let your pride get in the way - the possibility of the promise is too great!" So he did it. And he was healed - made completely clean. He claimed he had hope in the prophet by going to him in the first place. But it wasn't until he was asked to obey one very simple command that he was brought into the reality he was hoping for.

So it is in God's economy, we get to enjoy the blessings that attend those who walk with Him, only by actually walking with Him. The disciples would never have participated in the miracle of Jesus feeding the 5,000, if they hadn't obeyed His command to have the people sit down in groups, and carry the bread and the fish to them. They could have "said" they were His disciples, but their obedience demonstrated that it was true.

2. Baptism is a Demonstration of FAITH

Christians believe certain things in common. Not every Christian believes **everything** every other Christian believes, but there are some things which every Christian does believe along with every other Christian. Apart from believing these truths, we really can't call ourselves Christians. Among other things, true Christians all believe in the one true God who created the heaven and the earth. That this God is one being eternally existing in three persons - Father, Son and Holy Spirit. We believe in His only begotten Son, Jesus Christ - as both God and man. We believe the Bible is the Word of God. And we must believe the Gospel. For it is in believing in the Gospel - the good news that God punished Jesus Christ for human sin, so that all those who trust Christ as their substitute in bearing God's wrath for them - are forgiven all of their sin, reconciled to God, spared from the wrath to come, and given eternal life.

But how do we demonstrate that we really believe anything? We act on it. In essence, faith is believing that what God has said is true - and ordering our lives accordingly. If I really believe the message that my house is on fire - you'll know it, by the action I take. But if I don't really believe it, you'll know that too - by what I don't do.

So as we learn the things that baptism is meant to communicate to us, we demonstrate that we believe those things, by acting on them.

There are at least three key things that baptism demonstrates we believe God has revealed to us in His Word and that we place our faith in.

a. We believe that God's holy judgment upon sin in death, was taken by another - Jesus Christ at Calvary. And because we believe it is so we are baptized, demonstrating our faith in Him and symbolizing His death in our place, our union with Him in it and how we rise up to new life because He died in our place.

b. We believe that we have been buried with Him. That He truly died (it didn't just look like it) and we were buried with Him so that the sentence of death we were under is completely fulfilled. We are baptized to demonstrate we believe we can no longer be judged for our sin so as to suffer death and eternal separation from God. That is finished for us.

c. We believe and demonstrate our faith in the coming resurrection. The one who is baptized is demonstrating that they believe that as a Christian, they are joined together with all other Christians, and with Jesus Himself - identifying with our Lord and His people. This is why in 1 Corinthians 15 the apostle Paul says that baptism is really nonsense if there is no resurrection, for why in the world would we want to be identified with a bunch of people who are just dead and gone? But in baptism we demonstrate we believe those who died in Christ before us aren't just dead and gone, but that we are joined with Christ (and all believers) and will rise together when He comes.

3. Baptism is a Demonstration of having BELIEVED the Gospel.

While this is already touched on above, let's focus upon it a bit more here.

In Acts 8:35-38 we have the account of the "Ethiopian Eunuch." Having been to Jerusalem to worship, he is returning to Ethiopia when Phillip the evangelist hears him reading a passage from the prophet Isaiah. With the Spirit's prompting, Phillip goes over to him and asks him if he understands what he is reading. The passage reads: "Like a sheep he was led to the slaughter and like a lamb before its shearer is silent, so he opens not his mouth. In his humiliation justice was denied him. Who can describe his generation? For his life is taken away from the earth." (Acts 8:32–33 taken from Isaiah 53) We are told that Phillip began then at this very passage, to tell him the good news about Jesus Christ.

As they proceeded, the Bible says they came upon some water, and the man asked Phillip if he could be baptized. Phillip said: "If you believe with all your heart, you may." To which the Eunuch replied: "I believe that Jesus Christ is the Son of God." So Phillip baptized him then and there.

If we believe, when we believe - the natural, Biblical demonstration that we believe, is to be baptized.

III – What baptism DECLARES – What it says by our participating in it.

Symbols and signs are different means of saying something - communicating. When I got married, I gave my wife a ring, and she gave one to me. And to everyone who sees those rings on our hands, it says to them - even if we are nowhere near each other - that we are married persons. That we have entered into a relationship with commitments and vows and responsibilities and promises. The rings "say" this silently, but no less clearly and powerfully.

In fact, even before we were actually married, I gave what most men give their prospective brides in our culture - an engagement ring. And it seems that the picture of an engagement ring is a very helpful way of understanding baptism.

In believing the Gospel and committing ourselves to Christ, we receive from Him a token that marks us out as having entered into the discipleship relationship with Him. A relationship which just like marriage comes with commitments, vows, privileges and responsibilities tied exclusively to it. It makes one think of Paul's words in 2 Corinthians 11:2 where he tells believers he has "betrothed" them to one husband - and again of the marriage language used to refer to our final union with Christ after the resurrection.

There are a number of things which baptism declares, but let's look at just three.

1. Baptism Declares the ONCE-FOR-ALL nature of salvation.

One of the features of New Testament baptism is that it is never repeated. This is a wonderful way of making known the finished work of Christ on the Cross. He never needs to die again, and thus believers are saved once and for all.

> **Hebrews 7:27** says: *"He has no need, like those high priests, to offer sacrifices daily, first for his own sins and then for those of the people, since he did this once for all when he offered up himself."*

Baptism is a loud declaration that all the sinner needs for salvation has been provided in the once-for-all sacrifice of Jesus. We cannot lose our salvation any more than He can undo His death. It is done. And being done - it isn't like the types and shadows of His death in the sacrificial system of the Old Testament which are repeated. It is the fulfillment and it is complete. His blood is sufficient for ALL our sin, past, present and future. Nor do we need to get saved over and over again. Having trusted in Him and having been united to Him by faith, all that He did is applied to our account and cannot be undone, nor ever needs redone.

Baptism entered believingly - declares you ARE saved - NOW. Once you have come to Christ, you never have to fear that His work is in any way insufficient to see you through to the very end. The aspect of salvation in which you are made a new creature - is finished. Yes, you will still need to grow into the maturity of this new creature-hood - but you will never be more "saved" (justified, declared righteous in God's eyes) than the moment you first believed.

2. Baptism Declares the inward BAPTISM of the Spirit

When John the Baptizer was ministering in anticipation of Jesus' arrival, he spoke very clearly to this point.

> **Matthew 3:11** *"I baptize you with water for repentance, but he who is coming after me is mightier than I, whose sandals I am not worthy to carry. He will baptize you with the Holy Spirit and fire."*

John's baptism was a type and shadow of the work of Christ to come. The work that we are told in 1 Corinthians is at the very heart of our salvation and what it means to be a Christian:

> **1 Corinthians 12:12–13** *"For just as the body is one and has many members, and all the members of the body, though many, are one body, so it is with Christ. For in one Spirit we were all baptized into*

> *one body—Jews or Greeks, slaves or free—and all were made to drink of one Spirit."*

What makes us one with Christ and with all other believers, is that we have become partakers of the very same Holy Spirit who Christ poured out upon the Church. In fact, **Romans 8:9** says that anyone who does not have the Spirit of Christ is none of His - doesn't belong to Him. And,

> **Titus 3:5–7** *"he saved us, not because of works done by us in righteousness, but according to his own mercy, by the washing of regeneration and renewal of the Holy Spirit, whom he poured out on us richly through Jesus Christ our Savior, so that being justified by his grace we might become heirs according to the hope of eternal life.*

Baptism is specifically designed to declare these truths to all who witness it, and experience it. We have been baptized into one body, by the Spirit of Christ that he has given to us. Baptism declares this loudly and clearly.

3. Baptism Declares the MUTUALLY COMMITTED status of the Believer and Christ

Drawing again from the imagery of an engagement ring, baptism is a gift to believers as a sign that *"My beloved is mine, and I am His"* (**Song of Solomon 2:16a**).

What the ring declares to earthly engaged couples, baptism declares for those betrothed to Christ Jesus. He has made His unbreakable promise to marry us. To take us to Himself one day. To fulfill every promise by blessing us with Himself in the sweetest, most intimate and inexplicable glories of union with Him.

He gives the "ring" as the token or down payment of the final reality (see: Ephesians 1:14 where the Holy Spirit Himself is the guarantee of which baptism is the symbol). We accept the "ring" and say "yes!" in baptism. The mutual commitment sealed in a public declaration of our mutual love and impending union. Amazing. Baptism isn't for God, it is for us! These "declarations" are for you and me! It is our acceptance of the proposal to leave all others and cleave only to Him. He presents it to us as a gift and a token of His love, affection and intention to make us His bride.

V. Three Questions by way of application:

1. What about infants?

We've already addressed this question briefly above, but it might be good to note again here that Believer's Baptism is the unbroken New Testament Pattern: People "believed" and then they were baptized. There simply is no other pattern is ever given in the New Testament. The old patterns perished with the Old Covenant as they were fulfilled in the New. In examining all of the pertinent passages (Matt. 3:1-6; Acts 2:41, 8:12, 9:18, 10:47, 16:14, 16:34, 16:8) in every case, baptism is linked directly with a belief which came before the baptism, and never after.

As such, we conclude that infants are not the proper candidates for baptism, but only those who have already heard and believed the Gospel, trusting Christ for their salvation.

For a fuller discussion of the key issues in this debate among good brother sand sisters in Christ about infant baptism, see part II, and the appendices.

2. What about "re-Baptism"?

Perhaps you were one of those who was baptized as an infant, or older, but while still an unbeliever. The question for you might be "should I get re-baptized?"

Because we believe the Bible teaches Believer's baptism, we would say that no matter what ceremony you may have been a part of, you in fact haven't BEEN baptized at all. If one must BELIEVE in order to BE baptized, then simply being dunked, or sprinkled or poured on didn't baptize you - it just made you wet.

So the question really isn't should you be re-baptized? But rather should you be baptized in the first place? And if you are a believer in Jesus Christ, the answer is simple – yes!

However, we also have to bear in mind that many of our true brothers and sisters in Christ hold to the practice of infant baptism - believing they ARE fulfilling Christ's command or have fulfilled it.

And for one in Christ whose conscience is content with their baptism as an infant, we do not believe it necessary impose believer's baptism now - since Christian fellowship isn't based upon baptism but upon faith in Christ and following Him in holiness.

If one baptized as an infant however were come to think they were not baptized originally, we would hope any evangelical church would happily baptize them, but not "re-baptize" them.

3. What about those who have delayed?

Believers who have professed faith in Christ for some time - ought absolutely to consider taking the engagement ring of your Savior. It is a sweet and inexplicably wonderful gift to be received with humility and gratitude.

Lastly, a word to those children who have made a profession of faith - at least to your parents and so you come to the Lord's Table. Now is the time to think seriously about following Christ in baptism as well. If you are His by faith, then it is the Biblical and natural next step to enter into the fullness of that relationship in the way He has proscribed for all believers.

Believer's Baptism

PART II

The Debate – Digging Deeper

The brilliant 18th century theologian and preacher Jonathan Edwards wrote: "There is perhaps no part of divinity attended with so much intricacy, and wherein orthodox divines do so much differ as stating the precise agreement and difference between the two dispensations of Moses and Christ."[4]

He wasn't kidding. And the debate between "orthodox" believers and theologians over whether or not to baptize the infants of believing parents or believers only hinges on this very point.

In this debate over whether infant baptism is to be practiced in the New Covenant Church, or Believers' baptism only, we are in the final analysis dealing with two fundamentally different views of the Church. Each view grounded in a difference in understanding the "precise agreement and difference between the two dispensations of Moses and Christ."

Before we begin this portion then, we want to stress that this is an "in house" debate among true Christians with Biblical convictions. No one's salvation hangs on this question. Nor are the two opinions here in any way to be taken in such a way that either side denigrates the other, or imputes to heresy them.

The Church of Jesus Christ has discussed and debated this topic nearly since its inception. And many of those who hold the

---

[4] Jonathan Edwards, "Inquiry Concerning Qualifications for Communion," in The Words of President Edwards, 4 vols. 8th ed. (New York: Leavitt & Allen, 1858), 1:160.

opposite opinion of the one expressed and defended here are towering giants of holiness and devotion to Christ. Scholars and saints of the highest order. We disagree with their view on this topic - but we lock arms as fellow believers, lovers of Christ, defenders of the faith and those with whom we will spend eternity around the throne with our mutual Savior.

For those who feel the pains of this debate so sharply that they believe they must separate if not castigate those of the opposite view, we would heartily recommend (regardless of which side you may be on) a thorough reading of John Bunyan's extremely useful work "Differences in Judgment About Water Baptism—No Bar to Communion." In this profound treatise - among other things, the venerable Tinker of Bedford argues (in our opinion) forcefully and Biblically for union among all saints who differ on baptism.

That said, we respectfully submit the following 5 positive arguments for believer's only baptism, and 4 negative arguments against the baptism of the infants of believing parents. We qualify that last statement so as not to mischaracterize the orthodox, who would not approve of baptizing any infant but those of believers.

5 Positive arguments:

1. Believer's Baptism is the Unbroken NT pattern

2. Entrance into the New Covenant is expressly by the Holy Spirit

3. The Scripture descriptions of & denominations for The Church all incorporate terms of faith, belief & regeneration

4. Baptism inherently testifies to a completed work

5. The Promise in Acts2:39 is of the gift of the Holy Spirit - which is restricted to those whom

God shall call in every generation.

4 Negative Arguments:

1. Familial Solidarity - Evident under the Old Covenant, is expressly denied under the New Covenant

2. The so-called "Household" argument proves too much

3. Holy children in 1Cor.7:14 has no reference to baptism

4. There is no mention of it in the New Testament - period

5 POSITIVE ARGUMENTS:

1. Believer's Baptism is the Unbroken NT pattern: People believed, and were baptized. No other pattern is ever given anywhere in the New Testament. The old pattern perished with the Old Covenant.

A survey of all the pertinent passages leaves this without reasonable doubt, even when beginning with the baptism of John. We have emphasized certain salient points in the citations below.

Matt. 3:5-6 / *⁵ Then Jerusalem and all Judea and all the region about the Jordan were going out to him, ⁶ and they were baptized by him in the river Jordan, **confessing their sins.***

Acts 2:41 / *So **those who received his word were baptized**, and there were added that day about three thousand souls.*

Acts 8:12 / *But **when they believed** Philip as he preached good news about the kingdom of God and the name of Jesus Christ, they were baptized, both men and women.*

Acts 8:36-37 / *And as they were going along the road they came to some water, and the eunuch said, "See, here is water! What prevents me from being baptized?" And Phillip said, "**if you***

***believe** with all your heart, you may.* " *And he replied, "I believe that Jesus Christ is the Son of God."*

Acts 9:17–18 / *So Ananias departed and entered the house. And laying his hands on him he said, "Brother Saul, the Lord Jesus who appeared to you on the road by which you came has sent me so that you may regain your sight and be filled with the Holy Spirit." And immediately something like scales fell from his eyes, and he regained his sight. **Then** he rose and was baptized;*

Acts 10:44–48 / *While Peter was still saying these things, the Holy Spirit fell on all who heard the word. And the believers from among the circumcised who had come with Peter were amazed, because the gift of the Holy Spirit was poured out even on the Gentiles. For they were hearing them speaking in tongues and extolling God. Then Peter declared, "**Can anyone withhold water for baptizing these people, who have received the Holy Spirit just as we have?**" And he commanded them to be baptized in the name of Jesus Christ. Then they asked him to remain for some days.*

Acts 16:14–15 / *One who heard us was a woman named Lydia, from the city of Thyatira, a seller of purple goods, who was a worshiper of God. **The Lord opened her heart to pay attention to what was said by Paul. And after she was baptized**, and her household as well, she urged us, saying, "If you have judged me to be faithful to the Lord, come to my house and stay." And she prevailed upon us.*

Acts 16:32–34 / *"And **they spoke the word of the Lord to him and to all who were in his house**. 33 And he took them the same hour of the night and washed their wounds; and he was baptized at once, he and all his family. 34 Then he brought them up into his house and set food before them. And **he rejoiced along with his entire household that he had believed in God**."*

Acts 18:8 / *"Crispus, the ruler of the synagogue, **believed in the Lord, together with his entire household.** And many of the Corinthians **hearing Paul believed and were baptized**."*

In every case recorded, without exception, baptism was linked to understanding and faith in those being baptized. They understood their sin and the message regarding how it must be dealt with prior to their baptism. By knitting the passages together, we see that it was the Gospel, God, the Word of the Lord, etc. which was believed. Even in the case of John's baptism, his work reaches its zenith in proclaiming to those he is baptizing that it is Jesus Christ who is the Lamb who takes away the sin of the world. Nowhere do we ever find a single mention of anyone being baptized who was not believing themselves. Such then certainly is the case with infants who cannot yet believe.

2. The means of entrance into the New Covenant is expressly by the Spirit: No other way into the Church – properly denominated Christ's body ("baptized into one body") is ever alluded to in Scripture.

Galatians 3:25–29 *"But now that faith has come, we are no longer under a guardian, for in Christ Jesus you are all sons of God, through faith. 27 For as many of you as were baptized into Christ have put on Christ. 28 There is neither Jew nor Greek, there is neither slave nor free, there is no male and female, for you are all one in Christ Jesus. 29 And if you are Christ's, then you are Abraham's offspring, heirs according to promise."*

This passage in Galatians helps us understand the nature of the one-bodiedness of those "in Christ." What is to be noticed is:

a. All "in Christ Jesus" are "sons of God through faith".
b. All who were baptized into Christ have "put on Christ."
c. This oneness is due to being "in Christ Jesus".
d. As such, those in Christ are Abraham's offspring - or "heirs" according to the promise".

All of which Paul says in vs. 25 is the result of "faith" having come, and therefore no longer being under a guardian (in this place, the "guardian" being the Mosaic law).

Note how faith is the essential to being "in Christ Jesus" and therefore a part of the one Body of Christ.

1 Corinthians 12:12–13 *"For just as the body is one and has many members, and all the members of the body, though many, are one body, so it is with Christ. 13 For in one Spirit we were all baptized into one body—Jews or Greeks, slaves or free—and all were made to drink of one Spirit."*

Here again we see the foundational concept of the Body of Christ being "one" – by virtue of each member being baptized into the Body by the Spirit. The Spirit alone brings us into union with Christ and one another.

Hebrews 8:10–11 *"For this is the covenant that I will make with the house of Israel after those days, declares the Lord: I will put my laws into their minds, and write them on their hearts, and I will be their God, and they shall be my people. 11 And they shall not teach, each one his neighbor and each one his brother, saying, 'Know the Lord,' for they shall all know me, from the least of them to the greatest."*

Repeating the terms of the New Covenant (from Jeremiah 31), the writer to the Hebrews reminds us that all those within the Covenant have God's laws put into their minds and written upon their hearts, and that they each "know the Lord". This is central to our understanding of who is in covenant with God and who is not, from the vantage point of the New Covenant terms laid out in Scripture.

The Scripture simply does not describe anyone as being in the New Covenant apart from being a partaker of the Holy Spirit – who it is that baptizes us into Christ and into union with one another. New Covenant membership is utterly dependent upon the work of the Spirit in the individual. Nowhere in the Bible is anyone ever designated as a participant in the New Covenant apart from the Spirit of Christ.

3. The Scripture descriptions of and denominations for, The New Testament Church, all incorporate terms of faith, belief and regeneration, and never anything less.

a. **Hebrews 12:22–23** *"But you have come to Mount Zion and to the city of the living God, the heavenly Jerusalem, and to innumerable angels in festal gathering, 23 and to the assembly of the firstborn who are enrolled in heaven, and to God, the judge of all, and to the spirits of the righteous made perfect."*

b. **Galatians 3:23–27** *"Now before faith came, we were held captive under the law, imprisoned until the coming faith would be revealed. 24 So then, the law was our guardian until Christ came, in order that we might be justified by faith. 25 But now that faith has come, we are no longer under a guardian, 26 for in Christ Jesus you are all sons of God, through faith. 27 For as many of you as were baptized into Christ have put on Christ."*

c. **Ephesians 2:17–19** *"And he came and preached peace to you who were far off and peace to those who were near. 18 For through him we both have access in one Spirit to the Father. 19 So then you are no longer strangers and aliens, but you are fellow citizens with the saints and members of the household of God."*

d. **Romans 5:1–2** *"Therefore, since we have been justified by faith, we have peace with God through our Lord Jesus Christ. 2 Through him we have also obtained access by faith into this grace in which we stand, and we rejoice in hope of the glory of God."*

e. **Romans 8:9** *"You, however, are not in the flesh but in the Spirit, if in fact the Spirit of God dwells in you. Anyone who does not have the Spirit of Christ does not belong to him."*

There is no Scriptural support anywhere in the New Testament for denominating someone as in the Church, apart from personal belief, a confession of faith and sharing of the Holy Spirit. This does not mean the Church does not care for those who are not yet believers, especially our children. But it is our first task to evangelize them, not to treat them as though they are already in union with Christ. Union with Christ is only by the Spirit of Christ.

4. Baptism inherently testifies to a completed work and the promise fulfilled, whereas Circumcision only points to a future promise yet to be fulfilled.

This is not to say there is NO future concept expressed in baptism. Resurrection is also pre-figured as established above. However baptism is PRIMARILY looking backward to the already accomplished death, burial and resurrection of Christ. Our salvation is dependent upon a finished work in Christ at Calvary, not a work yet to be accomplished. Even the fulfillment of the resurrection is dependent upon the promises already fulfilled in Christ's death, burial and resurrection.

> **Romans 6:3** *"Do you not know that all of us who have been baptized into Christ Jesus were baptized into his death?"*

In contrast, circumcision was specifically given regarding a promise yet to be fulfilled, not, in regard to a promise already fulfilled. It was appropriate under the Mosaic Covenant, but not under the New Covenant.

> **Genesis 17:7–10** *"And I will establish my covenant between me and you and your offspring after you throughout their generations for an everlasting covenant, to be God to you and to your offspring after you. **8** And I will give to you and to your offspring after you the land of your sojournings, all the land of Canaan, for an everlasting possession, and I will be their God." **9** And God said to Abraham, "As for you, you shall keep my covenant, you and your offspring after you throughout their generations. **10** This is my covenant, which you shall keep, between me and you and your offspring after you: Every male among you shall be circumcised."*

> **Deuteronomy 30:6** *"And the LORD your God will circumcise your heart and the heart of your offspring, so that you will love the LORD your God with all your heart and with all your soul, that you may live."*

Note too, how circumcision is related directly to the inheritance promised to the Israelites. In their case, that promise was of land, which was meant to typify spiritual realities, not to be the final reality - something Abraham fully understood. (Heb. 11:10)

In the case of the New Covenant, the spiritual inheritance is the focus, and that, received by the giving of the Spirit. So we read in **Ephesians 2:11-19:**

> *"Therefore remember that at one time you Gentiles in the flesh, called "the uncircumcision" by what is called the circumcision, which is made in the flesh by hands— 12 remember that you were at that time separated from Christ, alienated from the commonwealth of Israel and strangers to the covenants of promise, having no hope and without God in the world. 13 But now in Christ Jesus you who once were far off have been brought near by the blood of Christ. 14 For he himself is our peace, who has made us both one and has broken down in his flesh the dividing wall of hostility 15 by abolishing the law of commandments expressed in ordinances, that he might create in himself one new man in place of the two, so making peace, 16 and might reconcile us both to God in one body through the cross, thereby killing the hostility. 17 And he came and preached peace to you who were far off and peace to those who were near. 18 For through him we both have access in one Spirit to the Father. 19 So then you are no longer strangers and aliens, but you are fellow citizens with the saints and members of the household of God,"*

We see clearly here that access to the Father, and the Covenant, is through the blood of Christ (already shed) and the Holy Spirit presently poured out (vss. 18-19). This is in stark contrast to the forward looking emphasis of circumcision under the Old Covenant.

5. The" Promise" referred to in Acts 2:39 is of the Holy Spirit, not the Covenant, and is restricted to those whom God shall call in every generation.

While it is often argued that Acts 2:39 supports the baptism of infants by stating: *"For the promise is for you and for your children and for all who are far off, everyone whom the Lord our God calls to himself."* It seems that perhaps 2 critical mistakes are made in that interpretation.

a. One must first determine what "promise" is being referred to here in the context of the passage. And there can be no exegetical doubt, the promise referred to is that of the giving of the Holy Spirit. In other words, the "promise" is not that children may have a part of the covenant through baptism – for baptism is not the subject of Peter's preaching. The pouring out of the Holy Spirit is Peter's topic, required by both the unusual phenomena of the day, and by Peter's express reference to the phenomena being directly related to the prophecy of Joel 2:28-32.

b. In addition, Peter's application is that the promise of the Holy Spirit is "for everyone whom the Lord God calls to Himself." The qualifying factor is having been called by God to Himself, not, simply being the children of believers. Yes, this promise is for all who believe, even the following generations and not that unique generation alone – but children or no, it is for those who are called by God to Himself.

This interpretation is confirmed by observing whom it was that manifested the Spirit on that day – the believers gathered and not the unbelievers. The Spirit was not indiscriminately poured out upon all the circumcised present. The Spirit is not given due to familial solidarity with the "covenant people" bearing the sign of circumcision, but to those among them who believed.

Verse 39 is prefaced by verse 38 – *"And Peter said to them, "Repent and be baptized every one of you in the name of Jesus Christ for the forgiveness of your sins, and you will receive the gift of the Holy Spirit."*

Those who repented and believed would receive the gift of the Spirit, and none else. The "promise" is of the Holy Spirit, and it is made to those who repent and believe. None other.

4 NEGATIVE ARGUMENTS:

1. Familial Solidarity –Evident under the Old Covenant, is expressly denied under the New Covenant.

The case is often made by our brothers and sisters who insist on infant baptism, that paedobaptism ought to be practiced as an expression of "familial solidarity" – a principle established by God in the giving of circumcision, establishing a lineage of promise and blessing.

Put simply, the idea is that God established a covenant with Abraham. God also gave a sign or a token of that covenant, which was circumcision. This sign was to be conferred upon all of Abraham's generations, marking them out as God's covenant people.

Based upon this solidarity which existed between all of the generations which issued from Abraham, the thought is that such a sign should still continue when we enter the New Covenant era. That since "God's people" (all the descendants of Abraham under the Abrahamic covenant) were to have the "sign" of that covenant, all the descendants of those in the New Covenant should have the "sign" of that covenant conferred upon them as well. We simply follow the pattern already established.

And before going any further, we must agree that the logic of the position is sound on the face of it. It makes sense. However, the question isn't whether or not the reasoning makes sense, but whether or not this connection between baptism and circumcision taken in this way is what the Bible teaches.

Two issues arise here which bear investigation in answering that question.

a. Does baptism in fact replace circumcision as the sign of the covenant? Did God institute water baptism as the sign of the New Covenant, in the same way that He established circumcision as the sign of the Old Covenant?

b. Does the Bible teach that the same principle of familial solidarity of passing the sign of the covenant on to natural offspring still apply under the terms of the New Covenant?

To the first question, we have to answer in the negative.

As noted in the first section of this book, Colossians 2:11 indicates that the "circumcision" of the New Covenant believer is one made "without hands", having been buried with Christ in baptism. Since the baptism referred to there is one made "without hands" we see that it cannot be water baptism which is being discussed but rather that baptism of the Spirit whereby we are placed into Christ (1 Cor. 12:13). The text itself clarifies that interpretation by adding that we were "raised with Him through faith". Faith is the operative agent here, not baptism as an act, which would be made "by" hands, as opposed to "without hands". In other words it is not a physical act which is being referred to. And water baptism is certainly a physical act.

To the second question we must also answer in the negative.

It appears that under the New Covenant, the familial solidarity evident under the Old Covenant and as manifested in circumcision is removed. We see evidence for this shift right from the very beginning of the New Testament.

So it is John Baptizer warns those coming to his baptism to be sure that they are not depending solely upon their familial connection with Abraham to be in full covenantal relationship with God:

> **Luke 3:8** *"Bear fruits in keeping with repentance. And do not begin to say to yourselves, 'We have Abraham as our father.' For I tell you, God is able from these stones to raise up children for Abraham."*

Family lineage – while it once carried the types and shadows of union with Christ, is seen to be set aside in favor of the fulfillment which had been typified. So John 1 marks out that being "children of God" is located in having believed in Christ's name and not somewhere else.

> **John 1:12-13** *"But to all who did receive him, who believed in his name, he gave the right to become children of God, who were born not of blood, nor of the will of the flesh nor of the will of man, but of God."*

Galatians 3 locates our familial connection to the family of believers in faith – not in circumcision or water baptism.

> **Galatians 3:26–29** *"for in Christ Jesus you are all sons of God, through faith. 27 For as many of you as were baptized into Christ have put on Christ. 28 There is neither Jew nor Greek, there is neither slave nor free, there is no male and female, for you are all one in Christ Jesus. 29 And if you are Christ's, then you are Abraham's offspring, heirs according to promise."*

1 Corinthians reminds us that the patterns in the Old Testament are types and shadows of the spiritual realities, and not the substance themselves. Therefore we are to expect a progression and

transition in the forms to those more representative of the realities. We start with physical things, but move on to spiritual things.

> **1 Corinthians 15:45–47** *"Thus it is written, "The first man Adam became a living being"; the last Adam became a life-giving spirit. 46 But it is not the spiritual that is first but the natural, and then the spiritual. 47 The first man was from the earth, a man of dust; the second man is from heaven."*

2. The "Household" argument proves too much.

The substance of this argument is that the Greek word *oikos* ("household" - used in such passages as Acts 16;15 where Lydia was baptized, "and her household as well") implies the entire household - including all family members, regardless of age. As such (those who take this position argue) there certainly might have been - if not MUST have been infants included in those numbers.

On the surface, the argument seems sound. But we must also bear in mind that the term *oikos* / household also went beyond that of spouses and progeny. As one resource defines it, oikos is defined as: "**family**, kin by blood or marriage, including slaves and workers [5]"

If (as proponents of infant baptism sometimes argue) one is *required* to assume that there were infants in the "household" references related to baptism in the New Testament, then we must also (if we are to remain consistent in our exegetical method) *require* that the slaves and workers in those households were also baptized - irrespective of age and/or profession of faith.

---

[5] Swanson, J. (1997). *Dictionary of Biblical Languages with Semantic Domains: Greek (New Testament)* (electronic ed.). Oak Harbor: Logos Research Systems, Inc.

With all due respect, we find this neither tenable nor desirable.

That it was "possible" that there were infants who must have been baptized is not a solid approach. Possibility is neither proof nor safe. It is possible that Balaam's ass spoke with Cajun accent. And according to the very same logic, it was possible that there were adult, unbelieving slaves or workers baptized as well. But there can be no proof and therefore it ultimately has no bearing whatever on the reality of how baptism is to be practiced.

3. Holy children in 1 Cor.7:14 has no reference to baptism.

> **1 Corinthians 7:14** *"For the unbelieving husband is made holy because of his wife, and the unbelieving wife is made holy because of her husband. Otherwise your children would be unclean, but as it is, they are holy."*

Three things are worthy of note here.

a. Whatever it is that is being said in this passage, this much is true - it is being said (at least contextually) irrespective of baptism. There is no reference to baptism in the passage, and therefore there can be no conclusion in regard to baptism drawn from it. Whatever happens here has no relation to baptism at all, but is only speaking of the relationships between a redeemed parent and their children, and their unredeemed spouse.

b. Whatever it is that is being said of the child of the believing parent, is also being said concerning the unbelieving spouse.

c. The main point appears to be: Just because you have come to the saving knowledge of Christ, do not imagine that you must separate either from your unconverted spouse nor your children. Believers are not defiled on their account, and the unconverted are in fact are benefitted by their connection to the saved.

For a believing Jew familiar with the account given in Ezra 10 and those Jews returning from the Babylonian exile and their marriages to gentiles - this could have raised significant issues in this regard. Paul quells them in this passage.

4. There simply is NO mention of infant baptism it in the New Testament. Period.

In fact, New Testament arguments are made which would be contradictory to infant baptism mindset. For example:

> **Galatians 6:15** *"For neither circumcision counts for anything, nor uncircumcision, but a new creation."*

If water baptism replaced circumcision, then what is said here about circumcision considered by itself must also be applied to baptism considered by itself. And what is said is - it does not count for anything. What DOES count? "A new creation."

> **Ephesians 2:11–13** *"Therefore remember that at one time you Gentiles in the flesh, called "the uncircumcision" by what I called the circumcision, which is made in the flesh by hands— 12 remember that you were at that time separated from Christ, alienated from the commonwealth of Israel and strangers to the covenants of promise, having no hope and without God in the world. 13 But now in Christ Jesus you who once were far off have been brought near by the blood of Christ."*

Circumcision was once the marker which separated the Jews from all the other races. As a result, Gentiles were "separated from Christ," "alienated from the commonwealth of Israel", "strangers to the covenants of promise", "having no hope", "and without God in the world." What changed that? Baptism? No. "You who once were far off have been brought near by the blood of Christ."

> **Philippians 3:3** *"For we are the circumcision, who worship by the Spirit of God and glory in Christ Jesus and put no confidence in the flesh—"*

The Believer's "circumcision" is not by virtue of baptism, but is located in worshiping by the Spirit of God, glorying in Jesus Christ and putting NO confidence in the flesh.

Recap:

Believer's Baptism is the Unbroken New Testament pattern.

Entrance into the New Covenant is expressly by the Spirit.

The Scripture descriptions of and denominations for "The Church" all incorporate terms of faith, belief and regeneration.

Baptism inherently testifies to a completed work.

The "Promise" in Acts 2:39 is of the Spirit – is restricted to those whom God shall call in every generation.

Familial Solidarity – a principle evident under the Old Covenant, is expressly denied under the New.

The "Household" argument proves too much.

"Holy children" in 1 Cor. 7:14 simply has no reference to baptism.

There is no mention of it in the New Testament. Period. Infant baptism simply is not taught in the New Testament, while Believer's Baptism clearly is.

We conclude then that the practice of infant baptism is one that is not taught in the Bible. And though there maybe be some reasonable and logical constructs which can be made to justify the practice, such constructs actually run counter to the way in which circumcision was abolished, by virtue of a circumcision made "without hands" - and not by water baptism.

Appendix A.

An excerpt from Spurgeon's Catechism-

Question 75 – What is Baptism?

Answer – Baptism is an ordinance of the New Testament, instituted by Jesus Christ (Mt 28:19) to be to the person baptized a sign of his fellowship with him, in his death, and burial, and Resurrection (Ro 6:3; Col 2:12), of his being in-grafted into him (Ga 3:27), of remission of sins (Mr 1:4; Ac 22:16), and of his giving up himself to God through Jesus Christ, to live and walk in newness of life (Ro 6:4,5).

Question 76 – To whom is Baptism to be administered? And to none other.

Answer - Baptism is to be administered to all those who actually profess repentance towards God (Ac 2:38; Mt 3:6; Mr 16:16; Ac 8:12,36, 37; 10:47,48), and faith in our Lord Jesus Christ,

Question 77 - Are the infants of such as are professing to be baptised?

Answer - The infants of such as are professing believers are not to be baptized, because there is neither command nor example in the Holy Scriptures for their baptism (Ex 23:13; Pr 6)

Appendix B.

A Short Catechism About Baptism

by John Tombes, B.D.

Heb 6.2. Of the Doctrine of Baptisms.

Luke 7.35. But Wisdom is justified of all her Children.

London: 1659

Edited by Dr. Michael T. Renihan, 1995. (Used with permission)

Slight emendations (in formatting and archaic words and spelling only) by Reid Ferguson, 2013.

John Tombes is a fascinating figure from the 17th century, and one uniquely suited to address this topic. An Anglican Churchman of some reputation, he came to be convinced to abandon the practice of paedobaptism and to adopt believer's baptism by an unnamed but "ingenious baptist" who knew his Bible well."

In time, Tombes debated some of the leading figures of his day on this topic - men like Richard Baxter. And he labored to have his position considered by the Westminster Divines before the Confession was codified, but to no avail.

While never actually leaving the Anglican communion, he nevertheless could not perform infant baptisms for conscience sake, and stepped away from the pastoral role while still supporting the Church.

Thoughtful, insightful and thoroughly Biblical, his work in this area remains at the forefront of those who had addressed the topic with all of its various facets and intricacies. His chief arguments remain (in this writer's opinion) unsatisfactorily answered by any opponent to this day.

We include this edition of his brief catechism on baptism as a wonderful reference in understanding the thought of those holding to believer's only baptism.

Quest. 1. Is baptism with water an ordinance of Christ, to be continued by his disciples till the end of the World?

Answer. Baptism with water is an ordinance of Christ, which is to be continued by his disciples till the end of the world; as appears by his command, Mat. 28.19,20. Mark 16.15,16. It is to be joined with preaching of the Gospel, and making disciples, by preaching, and teaching them to observe all that Christ commands; and so to be continued while these are to continue, which is proved to be till the end of the world, by Christ's promise of his being with them till then, which were vain, if the things appointed were not to be done so long.

Quest. 2. Is not the end of the world, as much as the end of the Age?

Answer. It appears that Matthew means by the end of the World, the last time, or day, wherein there will be a separation of good and bad, the one to be burned with fire, and the other to shine as the Sun, in that in the places wherein Matthew, uses the self-same form of speech (to wit Mat. 13.39,40,49. Mat. 24.3.) he cannot be understood to mean any other.

Quest. 3. May not the baptizing in Mat.28.19. Mark 16.16 be understood of some other baptism, than that of water?

Answer. The baptism there, must needs be understood of baptism by water, since baptizing, where ever it is made of John the Baptist's, or the disciple's act, which they did or were to do, is meant of baptizing with water, as John 4.1,2 and in many other places it appears; and the Apostles by their practice and command, Acts 2.38,41. Acts 10.47,48. show that they so understood Christ's appointment, Matt. 28.19. Mark 16.16.

Quest 4. May it not be meant of baptizing by the Spirit, or afflictions?

Ans. It cannot be so understood, since baptizing with the Spirit is nowhere ascribed to any other than Christ, Mat 3.11. Luke 3.16. Nor is baptism with the Spirit a duty for us to do, but a free gift of Christ; not common to all disciples of Christ, but peculiar to some: and to appoint them the baptizing by affliction had been to make the Apostles persecutors.

Quest. 5. Why did Paul then say, Christ sent him not to baptize? 1 Cor.1.16.

Ans. Not because he was not appointed at all to Baptize, for if so, he would not have baptized those he did baptize, 1 Cor. 1.14.16. etc. But because it was not the chief thing he was to do, as when the washing of water is said not to save, 1 Pet. 3.21. because it is not the only, or principal means of saving.

Quest. 6. What is the baptizing appointed by Jesus Christ?

Answer. The baptizing appointed by Jesus Christ, is the dipping of the whole body in water in the name of the Father, Son, and Holy Ghost, as is manifest from the term baptizing, and the use of going into and coming up out of water, Mat. 3.16. Acts 8.38,39. the use of much water, John 3.23. The resembling, by the baptism used, the burial and resurrection of Christ, Rom. 6.4. Col. 2.12. and the testimonies of the ancients of the first Ages.

Quest. 7. May not the sprinkling or pouring water on the face be the baptism of Christ?

Answer. Neither the Scripture, nor any other ancient author call sprinkling, or pouring water on the face, baptism, nor any use of it in the primitive times doth countenance it, and therefore such sprinkling or pouring water is not the baptism which Christ appointed.

Quest. 8. What is it to baptize into the name of the Father, Son, and Holy Ghost?

Answer. It is not to baptize only with the naming of those persons, but into the profession of the Father, Son, and Holy Ghost, as our Master or Teacher, as appears by the words of Paul, 1 Cor. 1.13. Which show that if the Corinthians had been baptized into the name of Paul, they had professed him to be their master.

Quest. 9. Are they rightly baptized, who are baptized into the name of Jesus Christ, though no other person be named?

Answer. They are, it being all one to baptize into the name of Jesus Christ, and to baptize into the name of the Father, Son, and Holy Ghost, as appears by the precept, Acts 2.38. and practice, Acts 10.48. Acts 19.5. Though the expression of each person be convenient.

Quest. 10. Are the persons to be baptized altogether passive in their baptism?

Answer. No: For baptism is their duty required of them as well as the baptizer, Acts 2.38. and Paul is commanded to arise and be baptized, and wash away his sins calling on the name of the Lord, Acts 22.16.

Quest. 11. Who are appointed to baptize?

Answer. They who are appointed to preach the Gospel, Matth. 28.19. Mark 16.15,16.

Quest. 12. Whom are they appointed to baptize?

Answer. Those who repent of sin, believe in Christ Jesus, and are his disciples, Matth. 28.19. Mark 16.16. Acts 2.38. Acts 8.37.

Quest. 13. Were not Infants baptized, when whole households were baptized, Acts 16.15.33.?

Answer. No: For it appears not there were any infants in the houses, and the texts show they were not baptized, since the word was spoken to all in the house, ver. 32. and all the house rejoiced believing God. Ver. 34. and elsewhere the whole house is said to do that which Infants could not do, Acts 18.8. Acts 10.2. 1 Cor. 16.15. compared with 1 Cor. 1.16. John 4.53.

Quest. 14. Is not Christ's speech and action to little Children, Matth. 19.14,15. Mark 10.14,15,16. Luke 18.16,17. a warrant to baptize infants?

Answer. No: but an argument against it, since Christ did neither baptize, nor appoint those little children to be baptized.

Quest. 15. Why should not Infants be baptized, since they were circumcised?

Answer. The reason why male infants were to be circumcised, was a particular command of God to Abraham's house for special ends belonging to the time before Christ, which baptism hath not, nor is there any command to use baptism according to the rule of circumcision.

Quest. 16. Did not baptism come in the room of circumcision, Col. 2.11,12. and so to be used as it was?

Answer. The Apostles words import not that our baptism came in the room of the Jews circumcision; there is no mention of any bodily circumcision but Christ's, which our baptism cannot be said to succeed to, as there it is made the cause of Spiritual Circumcision, without arrogating that to it which belongs to Christ alone, and baptism is mentioned with faith, as the means whereby we are in Christ, and complete in him.

Quest. 17. May we be said to be complete as the Jews without infant baptism?

Answer. Our completeness is in that we have not ordinances as the Jews had, but we are complete in that we have all in Christ without them, Col. 2.8,9,10.

Quest. 18. Have not our Children then less privilege than the Jews had?

Answer. No: For circumcision was a privilege only for a time, and comparatively to the estate of the Gentiles who knew not God; but of itself was a heavy yoke, Acts 15.10. Gal. 5.1,2,3.

Quest. 19. Why did the Jews then so much contend for it, Acts 15.1,5.

Answer. Because they too much esteemed the Law, and knew not their liberty by the Gospel.

Quest. 20. Had it not been a discomfort to the believing Jews to have their Children unbaptized, and out of the Covenant?

Answer. The want of baptism to infants was never any grievance to believers in the New Testament, nor were they thereby put out of the Covenant of Grace.

Quest. 21. Was not the proper reason of circumcising the Infants of the Jews the interest which they had in the Covenant to Abraham, Gen. 17.7. to be a God to him and to his seed?

Answer. The end of Circumcision was indeed to be a token of the whole Covenant made with Abraham, Gen. 17.4,5,6,7,8. not only the promise, ver. 7. But the formal proper distinguishing reason why some were to be circumcised, and others not, was God's command alone, not the interest in the covenant; since Ishmael who was not a child of promise, Gen. 17.20.21. Rom. 9.6,7,8,9. and those who were in Abrahams house, though not of his Seed, were circumcised, but no females, nor males under eight days old.

Quest. 22. Was not the covenant with Abraham, Gen. 17. the Covenant of Grace?

Answer. It was, according to the hidden meaning of the Holy Ghost, the Evangelical Covenant, Gal. 3.16. But according to the open sense of the words, a covenant of special benefits to Abraham's inheriting natural posterity, and therefore not a pure Gospel Covenant.

Quest. 23. Are not Believer's children comprehended under the promise, to be a God to Abraham and his seed? Gen. 17.7.

Answer. No: unless they become Abraham's seed according to election of grace by faith.

Quest. 24. Did circumcision seal the Gospel Covenant? Rom. 4.11.

Answer. That text speaks not of any one's circumcision but Abraham's, which sealed the righteousness of faith he had before circumcision, and assured thereby righteousness to all, though uncircumcised, who should believe as he did.

Quest. 25. Are not the sacraments of the Christian Church in their nature, seals of the Covenant of Grace?

Answer. The Scripture doth nowhere so call them, nor doth it mention this as their end and use.

Quest. 26. Does not Peter, Acts 2.38.39. exhort the Jews to baptize themselves and their children, because the promise of grace is to believers and their Children?

Answer. Those he then spoke to were not then believers; and therefore the words, Acts 2.39. cannot be understood of a promise to believers and their children as such, but the promise is to all, fathers and children as called of God; nor are any exhorted to baptism without fore-going repentance: nor is the promise alleged as conferring right to baptism, but as a motive to encourage them and hope for pardon, though they wished Christ's blood to be on them and their children. Matth. 27.25. In like sort as Joseph did, Gen. 50.19,20,21.

Quest. 27. Are not the children of believers holy with covenant-holiness, and so to be baptized, 1 Cor. 7.14.

Answer. There is nothing there ascribed to the faith of the believer, but to the marriage-relation, which was the only reason of their lawful living together, and of which alone it is true that all the children of those parents, whereof one is sanctified to the other, are holy, the rest unclean, that is, illegitimate.

Quest. 28. Are not the Gentile-believer's children to be ingrafted by Baptism with their parents, as the Jews children were by circumcision? Rom. 11.16,17.

Answer. The ingrafting there is by giving faith according to election; and therefore not meant of parents and children by an outward ordinance into the visible Church.

Quest. 29. Are there not infants of believers disciples, by their parent's faith to be baptized? Mat. 28.19. Acts. 15.10.

Answer. No: For the disciples there are only such as are made by preaching the Gospel to them, nor are any termed disciples, but those who have heard and learned: and the putting the yoke, Acts 15.10. was by teaching brethren, ver. 1 and therefore the disciples, ver. 10. not infants.

Quest. 30. Are not the infants of believers visible members of the Christian Church, by a law and ordinance, by God's promise, to be God to them and their seed, and precept to dedicate them to God, un-repealed?

Answer. There is no such ordinance or law extant in Scripture, or deducible from the Law of Nature, nor are infants anywhere reckoned as visible members of the Christian Church in the New Testament.

Quest. 31. Has God not promised, Gen. 22.16,17,18. to make every believer a blessing, so as to cast ordinarily elect children on elect parents, and thereby warrant infant baptism.

Answer. The promise does not pertain to any believer's seed but Abraham's, who are, Heb. 6.12,13,14, Gal. 3.8,9. Acts 3.25. expounded to be Christ and true believers only, who are to be baptized, not their Infants, till they themselves believe in their own persons.

Quest. 32. Did not Christ appoint, Mat. 28.19. the Disciples to baptize children with parents, as the Jews did proselytes?

Answer. If the Jewish baptism had been the pattern for Christians, the Apostles would have so practiced, but their not so doing, shows they understood not it to be Christ's mind.

Quest. 33. Is not the infant baptism sufficient if it be avouched at age?

Answer. It is not a sufficient discharge of their obedience to Christ's command, which requires each person to be baptized after his own repentance and believing in Christ, Mark 16.16. Mat. 28. 19. Acts 2.38. Ephes. 4.5.

Quest. 34. What is the chief end of Baptism.

Answer. To testify the repentance, faith, hope, love, and resolution of the baptized to follow Christ, Gal. 3.27. Rom. 6.3,4. 1 Cor. 15.29. calling upon the name of the Lord, Acts 22.16.

Quest. 35. How came infant baptism to be common in the Christian Churches?.

Answer. As infant communion came from mistake of John 6.53. so infant baptism began about the third age of the Christian Church, from mistake of John

3.5. The opinion of its giving grace, and the necessity of it to save the infant dying from perishing, and after Augustine's time became common, which before was not so frequent.

Quest. 36. Is there any evil in it?

Answer. Infant-baptism tends much to harden people in presumption, as if they were Christians afore they know Christ, and hinders much the reformation of Christian Churches, by filling them with ignorant and scandalous members, besides the great sin of profaning God's ordinance.

Quest. 37. Have not all opposers of infant baptism, been wicked in the end?

Answer. Blessed be God, experience proves the contrary, though some here to fore proved seditious, and entertained great errors.

Quest. 38. Is there any good by baptizing persons at age, which might not be, though infant baptism were continued?

Answer. Yes, For thereby they would be solemnly engaged to adhere to Christ, which is a strong tie on the consciences, when it is done by a person understandingly, according to Christ's mind, besides the assurance thereby of union and conformity to Christ, and Righteousness and life by him, Rom. 6.3,4. Gal. 3.26. 1 Pet. 3.21.

Quest. 39. What are Christians to do when they are baptized?

Answer. To associate together in Church-communion, and to walk according to their engagement, in obedience to them, who are over them in the Lord.

Quest. 40. Are persons so joined to separate from those they have joined to upon deficit in outward order and ordinances, or variation from the Rule therein by Pastors or people?

Answer. No, Unless the evil be such in faith, worship, or discipline, as is not consistent with Christianity, or the estate of a visible Church, or is intolerable oppression, maintained with obstinacy, after endeavors to cure them, to which end each member should keep and act in his station.

Appendix C.

Further Reading

1. Antipaedobaptism in the thought of John Tombes
Dr. Michael T. Renihan
Publisher: B & R Press (2001)

This invaluable volume is very hard to come by. Contacting Dr. Renihan through his church website would be my best advice. It is a profoundly interesting and useful work - unique in its material.
http://hbcma.org

2. Confirming our Faith: A Reformed Covenantal Theology of the Sacraments
Dr. KennethTalbot

Publisher: The Apologetics Group; 1ST edition (2009)
ISBN-10: 0977851664
ISBN-13: 978-0977851669

3. Baptism in the Early Church
H. F. Stander and J. P. Louw
Publisher: EP BOOKS (September 1, 2004)
ISBN-10: 0952791315
ISBN-13: 978-0952791317

The value of this slim volume is the research done on early Church baptism practices. Although the authors are paedobaptists, their thorough and honest work in Church history demonstrates that credobaptism - or professing believer's baptism was in fact the norm in the church at its earliest stages.

4. The Meaning and Mode of Baptism
Jay E. Adams
Publisher: P & R Publishing (January 1, 1992)
Language: English
ISBN-10: 087552043X
ISBN-13: 978-0875520438

This is another useful work in laying out the case for infant baptism in an orthodox and genial manner.

5. Differences in Judgment about Water Baptism, no Bar to Communion

John Bunyan

http://www.webrevival.net/en/books/bunyan/baptism.html

John Bunyan, the celebrated 17th century Baptist pastor, preacher and author of Pilgrim's Progress penned one of the most thoughtful, insightful, interesting and thought provoking papers on water baptism available. Arguing that our differing views about baptism (among the orthodox) ought to be no reason to keep earnest Christians from deep and close fellowship - he explores baptism in ways that few today ever consider. Agree or disagree with him, you will be challenged to think more deeply about how we stand on such issues (especially in debates between those holding to infant baptism and those holding to believer's only baptism) and the implications of our stand in terms of true Christian fellowship.

This paper is widely available on the web, and the address above is just one of many where it can be obtained.